The Value of Money

ONE DOLLAR
HOW MANY PENNIE$?

PORTIA SUMMERS

Enslow Publishing
101 W. 23rd Street
Suite 240
New York, NY 10011
USA

enslow.com

WORDS TO KNOW

bill—Paper money.

cent—What dollars are divided into. One hundred cents equal a dollar.

dollar—The currency of the United States.

mint—To create bills or coins.

symbol—An image that represents something else.

value—How much something is worth.

CONTENTS

A QUICK LOOK AT MONEY

penny
1¢

nickel
5¢

dime
10¢

quarter
25¢

half-dollar
50¢

one-dollar coin
$1

one-dollar bill
$1

five-dollar bill
$5

ten-dollar bill
$10

twenty-dollar bill
$20

HOW MUCH IS A PENNY WORTH?

A dollar is divided into cents.
The symbol for cents is ¢.
1 penny = 1¢

Find some pennies. Count 1
for each penny to find their
total value.
2 pennies = 2¢
5 pennies = 5¢

Five pennies have the
same value as one nickel.
5¢ = 5¢

HOW MANY PENNIES EQUAL A DIME OR A QUARTER?

Ten pennies are worth 10¢.
Ten pennies have the same value as one dime.
10¢ = 10¢

Moments in Minting

Pennies did not always look like they do today. This penny is from 1899.

Twenty-five pennies equal 25¢.
Twenty-five pennies have the same value as one quarter.
25¢ = 25¢

HOW MANY PENNIES EQUAL A HALF-DOLLAR OR A DOLLAR?

Fifty pennies equal 50¢.
Fifty pennies have the same value as a half-dollar.
50¢ = 50¢

One hundred pennies equal 100¢.
One hundred cents equal one dollar.
100¢ = $1.00
So one hundred pennies equal one dollar. A dollar can come as a coin, coins, or a bill.

HOW MUCH IS A NICKEL WORTH?

The value of a nickel is 5¢.
Find some nickels. Count them by 5s to find their total value.

5   10   15   20   25

2 nickels = 10¢
3 nickels = 15¢
4 nickels = 20¢
5 nickels = 25¢

HOW MANY NICKELS AND PENNIES EQUAL A DIME?
Two nickels add up to 10¢.
Two nickels have the same value as one dime.
10¢ = 10¢

Can you make 10¢ using nickels and pennies together? Count 5 for a nickel and 1 for each penny until you reach 10.

1 nickel + 5 pennies = 10¢

5   6   7   8   9   10

Moments in Minting

The nickel was first minted, or created, in the United States in 1866. President Thomas Jefferson hasn't always been on the nickel. The buffalo nickel has an American Indian on the front and an American bison on the back.

One nickel and five pennies have the same value as one dime.

10¢ = 10¢

HOW MANY NICKELS EQUAL A QUARTER?

Add nickels together to equal 25¢.
Count by 5s until you reach 25.

5   10   15   20   25

5 nickels = 25¢
Five nickels have the same value as one quarter.

HOW MUCH IS A DIME WORTH?

The value of one dime is 10¢.
Find some dimes. Count them by 10s to find their total value.

THERE IS A PATTERN

The number of dimes is the same number as the number in the tens place.

1 dime = 10¢
2 dimes = 20¢
3 dimes = 30¢
4 dimes = 40¢
5 dimes = 50¢

USING DIFFERENT COINS TO MAKE 10¢

1 dime = 10¢
2 nickels = 10¢
1 nickel + 5 pennies = 10¢
10 pennies = 10¢

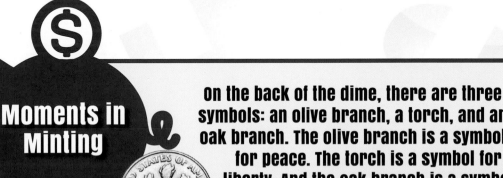

Moments in Minting

On the back of the dime, there are three symbols: an olive branch, a torch, and an oak branch. The olive branch is a symbol for peace. The torch is a symbol for liberty. And the oak branch is a symbol for strength.

HOW MUCH IS A QUARTER WORTH?

The value of a quarter is 25¢.

Find some quarters. Count them by 25s to find their total value.

Moments in Minting

The first coins were made 2,500 years ago. Ancient coins have been found in Europe, the Middle East, and Asia.

These coins are almost two thousand years old.

2 quarters = 50¢

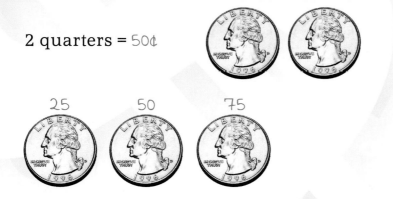

25   50   75

3 quarters = 75¢

HOW MANY DIMES AND NICKELS EQUAL A QUARTER?

Count 10 for each dime and 5 for each nickel until you reach 25.

10   15   20   25

One dime and three nickels are worth as much as a quarter.
1 dime + 3 nickels = 25¢

Two dimes and one nickel equal one quarter.
2 dimes + 1 nickel = 25¢

10   20   25

HOW MANY COINS EQUAL A DOLLAR?

You can write money amounts using a dollar sign ($) and a decimal point. One dollar is written as $1.00. As you know, one dollar equals 100 cents.

one-dollar bill = 100¢ = $1.00

There are many ways to make a dollar. The most common is the dollar bill.

There is also a dollar coin.

USE PENNIES TO MAKE A DOLLAR

It takes one hundred pennies to equal a dollar.

100 pennies = 100¢ = $1.00

USE NICKELS TO MAKE A DOLLAR

Count by 5s to reach 100.

You will find that twenty nickels equal a dollar.

20 nickels = 100¢ = $1.00

USE DIMES TO MAKE A DOLLAR

Count by 10s until you reach 100.

You will find that ten dimes equal a dollar.

10 dimes = 100¢ = $1.00

Moments in Minting

In math, the fraction ¼ means a quarter. This is how the quarter got its name. It is one quarter of a dollar.

USE QUARTERS TO MAKE A DOLLAR

Count by 25s until you reach 100.

25   50   75   100

You will find that four quarters equal a dollar.

4 quarters = 100¢ = $1.00

WHAT ARE THE VALUES OF DIFFERENT BILLS?

Five one-dollar bills are worth as much as a five-dollar bill.

1 five-dollar bill = $5.00
5 one-dollar bills = $5.00

Ten one-dollar bills or two five-dollar bills are worth as much as a ten-dollar bill.

1 ten-dollar bill = $10.00

2 five-dollar bills = $10.00

10 one-dollar bills = $10.00

USE DIFFERENT BILLS TO EQUAL $20

One twenty-dollar bill equals $20.00.

1 twenty-dollar bill = $20.00

Two ten-dollar bills equal $20.00.

2 ten-dollar bills = $20.00

Four five-dollar bills equal $20.00.

4 five-dollar bills = $20.00

Twenty one-dollar bills equal $20.00.
20 one-dollar bills = $20.00

One ten-dollar bill plus one five-dollar bill plus five
one-dollar bills equal $20.00.
1 ten-dollar bill + 1 five-dollar bill + 5 one-dollar bills =
$20.00

Two five-dollar bills plus one ten-dollar bill equal $20.00.
2 five-dollar bills + 1 ten-dollar bill = $20.00

How many other ways can you find to make $20.00?
How many different ways can you make $10.00? $5.00?
$1.00?

LEARN MORE

BOOKS

Cleary, Brian P. *A Dollar, a Penny, How Much and How Many?* Minneapolis, MN: Lerner Publications, 2015.

Domnauer, Teresa. *Money Mania Stick Kids Workbook*. Cypress, CA: Creative Teaching Press, 2012.

Marsico, Katie. *Money Math*. Minneapolis, MN: Lerner Classroom, 2015.

WEBSITES

H.I.P Pocket Change
www.usmint.gov/kids
Read about the history of the United States Mint, play games, and watch cartoons.

ABCYa.com
www.abcya.com/learning_coins.htm
Learn about US coins and dollar bills and play a sorting game.

INDEX

Published in 2017 by Enslow Publishing, LLC.
101 W. 23rd Street, Suite 240, New York, NY 10011

Copyright © 2017 by Enslow Publishing, LLC.
All rights reserved.

Library of Congress Cataloging-in-Publication Data
Names: Summers, Portia, author.
Title: One dollar : how many pennies? / Portia Summers.
Description: New York, NY : Enslow Publishing, [2017] | Series: The value of money | Includes bibliographical references and index.
Identifiers: LCCN 2015045457| ISBN 9780766076884 (library bound) | ISBN 9780766076853 (pbk.) | ISBN 9780766076860 (6-pack)
Subjects: LCSH: Dollar, American--Juvenile literature. | Coins, American--Juvenile literature. | Money--United States--Juvenile literature. | Counting--Juvenile literature.
Classification: LCC HG591 .Y43 2016 | DDC 332.4/040973--dc23
LC record available at http://lccn.loc.gov/2015045457

Printed in Malaysia

To Our Readers: We have done our best to make sure all websites in this book were active and appropriate when we went to press. However, the author and the publisher have no control over and assume no liability for the material available on those websites or on any websites they may link to. Any comments or suggestions can be sent by e-mail to customerservice@enslow.com.

Portions of this book originally appeared in the book *How Many Pennies Make a Dollar?* by Rebecca Wingard-Nelson.

Photo Credits: Cover (green dollar sign background, used throughout the book) Rachael Arnott/Shutterstock.com, Fedorov Oleksiy/Shutterstock.com; (white dollar sign background, used throughout the book) Golden Shrimp/Shutterstock.com; VIGE.COM/Shutterstock.com (piggy bank with dollar sign, used throughout book); Golden Shrimp/Shutterstock.com (green cross pattern border, used throughout book); p. 2 Africa Studio/Shutterstock.com; p. 3 John Brueske/Shutterstock.com; p. 4 penny (used throughout the book), mattesimages/Shutterstock.com; nickel (used throughout the book), United States Mint image; dime and quarter (used throughout the book), B. Brown/Shutterstock.com; half-dollar, Daniel D Malone/Shutterstock.com; one-dollar coin, iStock.com/JordiDelgado; one-dollar, five-dollar and twenty-dollar bills (used througout the book) Anton_Ivanov/Shutterstock.com; ten-dollar bill, Pavel Kirichenko/Shutterstock.com; p. 5 Girl counting, OJO_Images/iStockphoto.com; p. 6 1899 penny, tab62/Shutterstock.com; p. 7 Taylor Hinton/Thinkstock; p. 8 Buffalo nickel, Daniel D Malone/Shutterstock.com; p. 9 Frank van Delf/Cultura/Getty Images; p. 11 Polka Dot Images/Thinkstock; p. 12 Aleksei Gurko/Shutterstock.com, Samer.muhm/Shutterstock.com; p. 14 Fuse/Thinkstock; p. 18 JGI/Jamie Grill/Blend Images/Getty Images; p. 20 Lenora Gim/The Image Bank/Getty Images.